P9-CAS-820

AMERICAN CHRISTMAS

Edited by Webster Schott
and Robert J. Myers

# AMERICAN CHRISTMAS

Hallmark Cards, Incorporated
Kansas City, Missouri, 1965

Printed in the United States of America

Library of Congress Catalog Card Number: 63-13507

First Edition

Designed by K. K. Merker

A complete list of acknowledgements appears
at the end of this book.

## TABLE OF CONTENTS

William Cullen Bryant

## THE STAR OF BETHLEHEM

As shadows cast by cloud and sun
Flit o'er the summer grass,
So, in thy sight, Almighty One!
Earth's generations pass.

And while the years, an endless host,
Come pressing swiftly on,
The brightest names that earth can boast
Just glisten, and are gone.

Yet doth the Star of Bethlehem shed
A lustre pure and sweet;
And still it leads, as once it led,
To the Messiah's feet.

And deeply, at this later day,
Our hearts rejoice to see
How children, guided by its ray,
Come to the Saviour's knee.

O Father, may that Holy Star
Grow every year more bright,
And send its glorious beam afar
To fill the world with light.

Henry Wadsworth Longfellow,
translator

## CHRISTMAS CAROL

When Christ was born in Bethlehem,
'T was night, but seemed the noon of day;
    The stars, whose light
    Was pure and bright,
Shone with unwavering ray;
But one, one glorious star
Guided the Eastern Magi from afar.

Then peace was spread throughout the land;
The lion fed beside the tender lamb;
    And with the kid,
    To pasture led,
    The spotted leopard fed;
In peace, the calf and bear,
The wolf and lamb reposed together there.

As shepherds watched their flocks by night,
An angel, brighter than the sun's own light,
    Appeared in air,
    And gently said,
    Fear not,— be not afraid,
For lo! beneath your eyes,
Earth has become a smiling paradise.

*one of the* Neopolitan
Pastorali de' Zampognari

John Greenleaf Whittier

## A CHRISTMAS CARMEN

I

Sound over all waters, reach out from all lands,
The chorus of voices, the clasping of hands;
Sing hymns that were sung by the stars of the morn,
Sing songs of the angels when Jesus was born!
    With glad jubilations
    Bring hope to the nations!
The dark night is ending and dawn has begun:
Rise, hope of the ages, arise like the sun,
    All speech flow to music, all hearts beat as one!

II

Sing the bridal of nations! with chorals of love
Sing out the war-vulture and sing in the dove,
Till the hearts of the peoples keep time in accord,
And the voice of the world is the voice of the Lord!
    Clasp hands of the nations
    In strong gratulations:
The dark night is ending and dawn has begun;
Rise, hope of the ages, arise like the sun,
    All speech flow to music, all hearts beat as one!

III

Blow, bugles of battle, the marches of peace;
East, west, north, and south let the long quarrel cease:
Sing the song of great joy that the angels began,
Sing of glory to God and of good-will to man!
    Hark! joining in chorus

The heavens bend o'er us!
The dark night is ending and dawn has begun;
Rise, hope of the ages, arise like the sun,
All speech flow to music, all hearts beat as one!

Josiah Gilbert Holland

## A CHRISTMAS CAROL

There's a song in the air!
There's a star in the sky!
There's a mother's deep prayer
And a baby's low cry!
  And the star rains its fire while the Beautiful sing,
  For the manger of Bethlehem cradles a king.

There's a tumult of joy
O'er the wonderful birth,
For the virgin's sweet boy
Is the Lord of the earth,
  Ay! the star rains its fire and the Beautiful sing,
  For the manger of Bethlehem cradles a king.

In the light of that star
Lie the ages impearled;
And that song from afar
Has swept over the world.
  Every hearth is aflame, and the Beautiful sing,
  In the homes of the nations that Jesus is King.

We rejoice in the light,
And we echo the song
That comes down through the night
From the heavenly throng.
  Ay! we shout to the lovely evangel they bring,
  And we greet in His cradle our Saviour and King.

James Russell Lowell

## A CHRISTMAS CAROL

*For the Sunday-school Children of the Church of the Disciples*

"What means this glory round our feet,"
The Magi mused, "more bright than morn?"
And voices chanted clear and sweet,
"To-day the Prince of Peace is born!"

"What means that star," the Shepherds said,
"That brightens through the rocky glen?"
And angels, answering overhead,
Sang, "Peace on earth, good-will to men!"

'T is eighteen hundred years and more
Since those sweet oracles were dumb;
We wait for Him, like them of yore;
Alas, He seems so slow to come!

But it was said, in words of gold
No time or sorrow e'er shall dim,
That little children might be bold
In perfect trust to come to Him.

All round about our feet shall shine
A light like that the wise men saw,
If we our loving wills incline
To that sweet Life which is the Law.

So shall we learn to understand
The simple faith of shepherds then,
And, clasping kindly hand in hand,
Sing, "Peace on earth, good-will to men!"

And they who do their souls no wrong,
But keep at eve the faith of morn,
Shall daily hear the angel-song,
"To-day the Prince of Peace is born!"

Emily Dickinson

## CHRIST'S BIRTHDAY

The Savior must have been
A docile Gentleman
To come so far, so cold a day
For little fellowmen.

The road to Bethlehem
Since He and I were boys
Was leveled, but for that 'twould be
A rugged billion miles.

Richard Watson Gilder

## A CHRISTMAS HYMN

Tell me what is this innumerable throng
Singing in the heavens a loud angelic song?
*These are they who come with swift and shining feet*
*From round about the throne of* God *the* Lord *of* Light *to greet.*

O, who are these that hasten beneath the starry sky,
As if with joyful tidings that through the world shall fly?
*The faithful shepherds these, who greatly were afeared*
*When, as they watched their flocks by night, the heavenly host appeared.*

Who are these that follow across the hills of night
A star that westward hurries along the fields of light?
*Three wise men from the east who myrrh and treasure bring*
*To lay them at the feet of him their* Lord *and* Christ *and* King.

What babe new-born is this that in a manger cries?
Near on her bed of pain his happy mother lies?
O, *see! the air is shaken with white and heavenly wings—*
*This is the* Lord *of all the earth, this is the* King *of* Kings.

Tell me, how may I join in this holy feast
With all the kneeling world, and I of all the least?
*Fear not,* O *faithful heart, but bring what most is meet:*
*Bring love alone, true love alone, and lay it at his feet.*

James Whitcomb Riley

## THE CHRISTMAS LONG AGO

Come, sing a hale Heigh-ho
  For the Christmas long ago!—
When the old log-cabin homed us
    From the night of blinding snow,
  Where the rarest joy held reign,
  And the chimney roared amain,
With the firelight like a beacon
    Through the frosty window-pane.

  Ah! the revel and the din
  From without and from within,
The blend of distant sleigh-bells
    With the plinking violin;
  The muffled shrieks and cries—
  Then the glowing cheeks and eyes—
The driving storm of greetings,
    Gusts of kisses and surprise.

Eugene Field

## CHRISTMAS EVE

Oh hush thee, little Dear-my-soul,
The evening shades are falling,—
Hush thee, my dear, dost thou not hear
The voice of the Master calling?

Deep lies the snow upon the earth,
But all the sky is ringing
With joyous song, and all night long
The stars shall dance, with singing.

Oh hush thee, little Dear-my-soul,
And close thine eyes in dreaming,
And angels fair shall lead thee where
The singing stars are beaming.

A shepherd calls his little lambs,
And he longeth to caress them;
He bids them rest upon his breast,
That his tender love may bless them.

So hush thee, little Dear-my-soul,
Whilst evening shades are falling,
And above the song of the heavenly throng
Thou shalt hear the Master calling.

Edwin Markham

## THE SONG OF THE MAGI

*"Now when Jesus was born in Bethlehem ... behold, there came wise men from the east to Jerusalem.... And, lo, the star, which they saw in the east, went before them, till it came and stood over where the young child was.... And being warned of God in a dream ... they departed into their own country another way."*—Matthew

With a burning in our spirits, with a lifting of our hands,
We have threaded fallen kingdoms long forgotten in the sands–
Dead kingdoms where the thistles crowd to guard the empty
 thrones,
Where lone owls hoot their loud disdain among the scattered
 stones.
We passed the ghost of Nineveh upon the windy waste,
Where once the Angel of the Sword the paths of Eden paced.
We trod on crumbled Babylon, where once on towered hight
Her wingéd lions watched away the lone Assyrian night.
Out of the hush of the holy East, out of the night of old,
We seek the One the keepers of the sacred fire foretold.
Long centuries the wise have watched upon a peak afar,
Twelve Magi keeping vigil for the rising of the star.
Long ages they have waited for the herald of the birth,
The great hour when a Child should rise to poise the shaken
 earth.

We come commanded by a star and sent by dream we go;
Yet of this hour hereafter all the worlds and heavens shall know
This is the One we worship in the splendor of the fire:
He is the dream of every heart, he is the world's desire.
The prophet watchers cried of him with vision-lighted eyes:

They saw his scepter hush the earth and lean against the skies.
'Twas he the Vedic poets sang in ages that are gone,
The fair young God they knelt to in the brightness of the dawn.
This is the Golden Child that rose when worlds began to be,
And floated in the lotus flower upon the mother Sea.
This is the Child of Mystery drawn down to earthly years,
To bear the common burden and to taste of mortal tears.

Lizette Woodworth Reese

## A CHRISTMAS FOLK SONG

The little Jesus came to town;
The wind blew up, the wind blew down;
Out in the street the wind was bold;
Now who would house Him from the cold?

Then opened wide a stable door,
Fair were the rushes on the floor;
The Ox put forth a hornèd head;
"Come, little Lord, here make Thy bed."

Uprose the Sheep were folded near:
"Thou Lamb of God, come, enter here."
He entered there to rush and reed,
Who was the Lamb of God indeed.

The little Jesus came to town;
With ox and sheep He laid Him down;
Peace to the byre, peace to the fold,
For they housed Him from the cold!

Katharine Lee Bates

## THE LAME SHEPHERD

Slowly I followed on,
Stumbling and falling.
All the air sparkled;
All the air sung.
Even to my dull heart
Glory was calling.
Slowly I followed on,
Stumbling and falling.

Great wings arched over me,
Purple and amber;
Night was all color,
Night was all gleam.
Wearily up the hill
Needs must I clamber,
Though wings arched over me,
Purple and amber.

Proudly the chorus pealed
While I was panting.
Winds were all music,
Voices all praise.
Brooks, birds, the waving trees
Joined in the chanting.
Proudly the chorus pealed
While I was panting.

Late came my aching feet,
Late to the manger;

All slept in silence,
All dreamed in dusk
Under the same dear stars,
No star a stranger.
Late came my aching feet,
Late to the manger.

Kissing a baby's hand,
Painfully kneeling,
Sweet little drowsy hand,
Honey of heaven,
Swift through my twisted limbs
Glowed a glad healing.
Kissing a baby's hand,
Kissing and healing.

Langdon E. Mitchell

## CAROL

Mary, the mother, sits on the hill,
And cradles Child Jesu, that lies so still;
She cradles Child Jesu, that sleeps so sound,
And the little wind blows the song around.

The little wind blows the mother's words,
"Ei, Jesu, ei," like the song of birds;
"Ei, Jesu, ei," I heard it still,
As I lay asleep at the foot of the hill.

"Sleep, Babe, sleep, mother watch doth keep,
Ox shall not hurt Thee, nor ass, nor sheep;
Dew falls sweet from Thy Father's sky
Sleep, Jesu, sleep! ei, Jesu, ei."

Robert Frost

## TO A YOUNG WRETCH

*(Boethian)*

As gay for you to take your father's ax
As take his gun—rod—to go hunting—fishing.
You nick my spruce until its fiber cracks,
It gives up standing straight and goes down swishing.
You link an arm in its arm and you lean
Across the light snow homeward smelling green.

I could have bought you just as good a tree
To frizzle resin in a candle flame,
And what a saving 'twould have meant to me.
But tree by charity is not the same
As tree by enterprise and expedition.
I must not spoil your Christmas with contrition.

It is your Christmases against my woods.
But even where thus opposing interests kill,
They are to be thought of as opposing goods
Oftener than as conflicting good and ill;
Which makes the war god seem no special dunce
For always fighting on both sides at once.

And though in tinsel chain and popcorn rope,
My tree a captive in your window bay
Has lost its footing on my mountain slope
And lost the stars of heaven, may, oh, may
The symbol star it lifts against your ceiling
Help me accept its fate with Christmas feeling.

Carl Sandburg

## STAR SILVER

The silver of one star
Plays cross-lights against pine green.

And the play of this silver
Crosswise against the green
Is an old story... thousands of years.

And sheep raisers on the hills by night
Watching the wooly four-footed ramblers,
Watching a single silver star—
Why does the story never wear out?

And a baby slung in a feed-box
Back in a barn in a Bethlehem slum,
A baby's first cry mixing with the crunch
Of a mule's teeth on Bethlehem Christmas corn,
Baby fists softer than snowflakes of Norway,
The vagabond mother of Christ
And the vagabond men of wisdom,
All in a barn on a winter night,
And a baby there in swaddling clothes on hay—
Why does the story never wear out?

The sheen of it all
Is a star silver and a pine green
For the heart of a child asking a story,
The red and hungry, red and hankering heart
Calling for cross-lights of silver and green.

Don Marquis

## THE BIRTH

There is a legend that the love of God
So quickened under Mary's heart it wrought
Her very maidenhood to holier stuff....
However that may be, the birth befell
Upon a night when all the Syrian stars
Swayed tremulous before one lordlier orb
That rose in gradual splendor,
Paused,
Flooding the firmament with mystic light,
And dropped upon the breathing hills
A sudden music
Like a distillation from its gleams;
A rain of spirit and a dew of song!

Vachel Lindsay

## STAR OF MY HEART

Star of my heart, I follow from afar.
Sweet Love on high, lead on where shepherds are,
Where Time is not, and only dreamers are.
Star from of old, the Magi-Kings are dead
And a foolish Saxon seeks the manger-bed.
O lead me to Jehovah's child
Across this dreamland lone and wild,
Then I will speak this prayer unsaid,
And kiss his little haloed head—
"My star and I, we love thee, little child."

Except the Christ be born again to-night
In dreams of all men, saints and sons of shame,
The world will never see his kingdom bright.
Star of all hearts, lead onward thro' the night
Past death-black deserts, doubts without a name,
Past hills of pain and mountains of new sin
To that far sky where mystic births begin,
Where dreaming ears the angel-song shall win.
Our Christmas shall be rare at dawning there,
And each shall find his brother fair,
Like a little child within:
All hearts of the earth shall find new birth
And wake, no more to sin.

William Carlos Williams

## THE GIFT

As the wise men of old brought gifts<br>
  guided by a star<br>
    to the humble birthplace

of the god of love,<br>
  the devils<br>
    as an old print shows<br>
retreated in confusion.

  What could a baby know<br>
    of gold ornaments<br>
or frankincense and myrrh,<br>
  of priestly robes<br>
    and devout genuflections?

But the imagination<br>
  knows all stories<br>
    before they are told<br>
and knows the truth of this one<br>
  past all defection.

The rich gifts<br>
  so unsuitable for a child<br>
    though devoutly proffered,<br>
stood for all that love can bring.<br>
  The men were old<br>
    how could they know

of a mother's needs

or a child's
appetite?

But as they kneeled
the child was fed.
They saw it
and
gave praise!
A miracle

had taken place,
hard gold to love,
a mother's milk!
before
their wondering eyes.

The ass brayed
the cattle lowed.
It was their nature.
All men by their nature give praise.
It is all
they can do.

The very devils
by their flight give praise.
What is death,
beside this?
Nothing. The wise men
came with gifts

and bowed down
to worship
this perfection.

Sara Teasdale

## CHRISTMAS CAROL

The kings they came from out the south,
All dressed in ermine fine;
They bore Him gold and chrysoprase,
And gifts of precious wine.

The shepherds came from out the north,
Their coats were brown and old;
They brought Him little new-born lambs—
They had not any gold.

The wise men came from out the east,
And they were wrapped in white;
The star that led them all the way
Did glorify the night.

The angels came from heaven high,
And they were clad with wings;
And lo, they brought a joyful song
The host of heaven sings.

The kings they knocked upon the door,
The wise men entered in,
The shepherds followed after them
To hear the song begin.

The angels sang through all the night
Until the rising sun,
But little Jesus fell asleep
Before the song was done.

Louis Untermeyer

## FOR ANOTHER BIRTH

The miracle is now. The place is here.
No angel's wings. No throne. No diadem.
Yet, in this hour locked and rocked with fear,
A birth may mark another Bethlehem.

No kings surround a cradle. Crowds roar by.
The shepherds have been missing since the war.
Yet darkness splinters as a wintry sky
Unfolds and holds—again—a burning star.

This is a time for wonders. The world cries
For revelation, for another birth.
Dry sticks burst into blossom; dead bones rise;
And prophets whisper to a desperate earth.

Some child unborn may rescue us, for still
The wise men come with promise of release:
The myrrh of hope, the gold of men's good will,
The fresh and precious frankincense of peace.

Welcome all saints, all saviors of all time.
Welcome the thorns on every martyr's brow.
Welcome the cross. Welcome the long, slow climb.
The place is here. The miracle is now.

Joyce Kilmer

## GATES AND DOORS

*A Ballad of Christmas Eve*

There was a gentle hostler
    (And blessèd be his name!)
He opened up the stable
    The night Our Lady came.
Our Lady and Saint Joseph,
    He gave them food and bed,
And Jesus Christ has given him
    A glory round his head.

*So let the gate swing open*
    *However poor the yard,*
*Lest weary people visit you*
    *And find their passage barred;*
*Unlatch the door at midnight*
    *And let your lantern's glow*
*Shine out to guide the traveler's feet*
    *To you across the snow.*

There was a courteous hostler
    (He is in Heaven tonight,)
He held Our Lady's bridle
    And helped her to alight;
He spread clean straw before her
    Whereon she might lie down,
And Jesus Christ has given him
    An everlasting crown.

*Unlock the door this evening*
*And let your gate swing wide,*
*Let all who ask for shelter*
*Come speedily inside.*
*What if your yard be narrow?*
*What if your house be small?*
*There is a Guest is coming*
*Will glorify it all.*

There was a joyous hostler
Who knelt on Christmas morn
Beside the radiant manger
Wherein his Lord was born.
His heart was full of laughter,
His soul was full of bliss
When Jesus, on His Mother's lap,
Gave him His hand to kiss.

*Unbar your heart this evening*
*And keep no stranger out,*
*Take from your soul's great portal*
*The barrier of doubt.*
*To humble folk and weary*
*Give hearty welcoming,*
*Your breast shall be tomorrow*
*The cradle of a King.*

Elizabeth Madox Roberts

## CHRISTMAS MORNING

If Bethlehem were here today,
Or this were very long ago,
There wouldn't be a winter time
Nor any cold or snow.

I'd run out through the garden gate,
And go down along the pasture walk;
And off beside the cattle barns
I'd hear a kind of gentle talk.

I'd move the heavy iron chain
And pull away the wooden pin;
I'd push the door a little bit
And tiptoe very softly in.

The pigeons and the yellow hens
And all the cows would stand away;
Their eyes would open wide to see
A lady in the manger hay,

If this were very long ago
And Bethlehem were here today.

And Mother held my hand and smiled—
I mean the lady would—and she
Would take the woolly blankets off
Her little boy so I could see.

His shut-up eyes would be asleep,
And he would look like our John,
And he would be all crumpled too,
And have a pinkish color on.

I'd watch his breath go in and out.
His little clothes would all be white.
I'd slip my finger in his hand
To feel how he could hold it tight.

And she would smile and say, "Take care,"
The mother, Mary, would, "Take care,"
And I would kiss his little hand
And touch his hair.

While Mary put the blankets back,
The gentle talk would soon begin.
And when I'd tiptoe softly out
I'd meet the wise men going in.

Robinson Jeffers

## ONLY AN HOUR

For an hour on Christmas Eve
And again on the holy day
Seek the magic of past time,
From this present turn away.
Dark though our day,
Light is the snow on the hawthorn bush
And the ox knelt down at midnight.

Only an hour, only an hour
From wars and confusions turn away
To the islands of old time
When the world was simple and gay,
Or so we say,
And light lay the snow on the green holly,
The tall oxen knelt at midnight

Caesar and Herod shared the world,
Sorrow over Bethlehem lay,
Iron the empire, brutal the time,
Dark was that day,
Light lay the snow on the mistletoe berries
And the ox knelt down at midnight.

Sister M. Madeleva, C. S. C.

## PERENNIAL

The final wild song of Your birth-night
can never be written;
The last shining word of Your coming
can not be said.
Rough, slow-minded shepherds will run,
angel-driven, forever
By night to a cave and a cattle shed.

And You, beyond bondage of time, without
end or beginning,
Will wake in the arms of a maid,
on an unending night.
You the unuttered Word become Flesh
and forever now spoken,
Will be here, be our Life, our
accessible Light.

Tonight is Your night, Your incredible,
song-spangled story.
We shepherds and flocks wait on fields
beyond Bethlehem plain;
O angels, O shepherds, O Joseph, O Mary,
O Jesus,
O God, tell Your children the story again!

T.S. Eliot

## JOURNEY OF THE MAGI

'A cold coming we had of it,
Just the worst time of the year
For a journey, and such a long journey:
The ways deep and the weather sharp,
The very dead of winter.'
And the camels galled, sore-footed, refractory,
Lying down in the melting snow.
There were times we regretted
The summer palaces on slopes, the terraces,
And the silken girls bringing sherbet.
Then the camel men cursing and grumbling
And running away, and wanting their liquor and women,
And the night-fires going out, and the lack of shelters,
And the cities hostile and the towns unfriendly
And the villages dirty and charging high prices:
A hard time we had of it.
At the end we preferred to travel all night,
Sleeping in snatches,
With the voices singing in our ears, saying
That this was all folly.

Then at dawn we came down to a temperate valley,
Wet, below the snow line, smelling of vegetation;
With a running stream and a water-mill beating the dark
And three trees on the low sky,
And an old white horse galloped away in the meadow.
Then we came to a tavern with vine-leaves over the lintel,
Six hands at an open door dicing for pieces of silver,
And feet kicking the empty wine-skins.

But there was no information, and so we continued
And arrived at evening, not a moment too soon
Finding the place; it was (you may say) satisfactory.

All this was a long time ago, I remember,
And I would do it again, but set down
This set down
This: were we led all that way for
Birth or Death? There was a Birth, certainly,
We had evidence and no doubt. I had seen birth and death,
But had thought they were different; this Birth was
Hard and bitter agony for us, like Death, our death.
We returned to our places, these Kingdoms,
But no longer at ease here, in the old dispensation,
With an alien people clutching their gods.
I should be glad of another death.

Conrad Aiken

## CHRISTMAS EVE

Between the snowflake and the star
among the falling grains of sand
the interval of near or far
from Avatar to Samarkand

and voices on the midnight blown
and laughter in the sunlight gone
the jewel fallen from a throne
and ashes on a sill at dawn

as of the unseen in the seen
and of the unheard in the heard
the meaning that we almost mean
the truth within the broken word

in these is our epiphany
the pebble on the crucial road
the thorn upon the breaking tree
the back that bends beneath the load

and it is time we turned again
toward the window of the soul
where daybreak brings its sure amen
from the vast vista of the Whole.

Edna St. Vincent Millay

## TO JESUS ON HIS BIRTHDAY

For this your mother sweated in the cold,
For this you bled upon the bitter tree:
A yard of tinsel bought and sold;
A paper wreath; a day at home for me.
The merry bells ring out, the people kneel;
Up goes the man of God before the crowd;
With voice of honey and with eyes of steel
He drones your humble gospel to the proud.
Nobody listens. Less than the wind that blows
Are all your words to us you died to save.
O Prince of Peace! O Sharon's dewy Rose!
How mute you lie within your vaulted grave.
  The stone the angel rolled away with tears
  Is back upon your mouth these thousand years.

Archibald MacLeish

## THE SNOW FALL

Quietness clings to the air.
Quietness gathers the bell
To a great distance.
Listen!
This is the snow.
This is the slow
Chime
The snow
Makes.
It encloses us.
Time in the snow is alone:
Time in the snow is at last,
Is past.

E. E. Cummings

## LITTLE TREE

little tree
little silent Christmas tree
you are so little
you are more like a flower

who found you in the green forest
and were you very sorry to come away?
see      i will comfort you
because you smell so sweetly

i will kiss your cool bark
and hug you safe and tight
just as your mother would,
only don't be afraid

look      the spangles
that sleep all the year in a dark box
dreaming of being taken out and allowed to shine,
the balls the chains red and gold the fluffy threads,

put up your little arms
and i'll give them all to you to hold
every finger shall have its ring
and there won't be a single place dark or unhappy

then when you're quite dressed
you'll stand in the window for everyone to see
and how they'll stare!
oh but you'll be very proud

and my little sister and i will take hands
and looking up at our beautiful tree
we'll dance and sing
"Noel Noel"

Mark Van Doren

## DIALOGUE IN DECEMBER

In so much dark no light is little.
    But can light be at the end of the year?
Only listen. It will come.
    And put out dying? And put out fear?
Yes, but listen good heart, listen.
    I do, I do—I see, I hear.
That star is enough in this much night.
    It glitters. But a child has cried.
He is the first one in the world.
    Even the old world, that died?
Even the new—he is all the living.
    And all the dead—are they satisfied?

Listen and look—is there any weeping?
    Only for comfort, only for joy.
Only for love. But the child that was crying—
    He is a beautiful, strange boy.
He is little and weak, this lord of the world.
    But oh, too strong, too strong to destroy.

Allen Tate

## SONNETS AT CHRISTMAS

### II

Ah, Christ, I love you rings to the wild sky
And I must think a little of the past:
When I was ten I told a stinking lie
That got a black boy whipped; but now at last
The going years, caught in an accurate glow,
Reverse like balls englished upon green baize—
Let them return, let the round trumpets blow
The ancient crackle of the Christ's deep gaze.

Deafened and blind, with senses yet unfound,
Am I, untutored to the after-wit
Of knowledge, knowing a nightmare has no sound;
Therefore with idle hands and head I sit
In late December before the fire's daze
Punished by crimes of which I would be quit.

Langston Hughes

## CHRISTMAS EVE

*Nearing Midnight in New York*

The Christmas trees are almost all sold
And the ones that are left go cheap.
The children almost all over town
Have almost gone to sleep.

The skyscraper lights on Christmas Eve
Have almost all gone out.
There's very little traffic,
Almost no one about.

Our town's almost as quiet
As Bethlehem must have been
Before a sudden angel chorus
Sang PEACE ON EARTH!
GOOD WILL TO MEN!

Our old Statue of Liberty
Looks down almost with a smile
As the Island of Manhattan
Awaits the morning of the Child.

Phyllis McGinley

## THE BALLAD OF BEFANA

*An Epiphany Legend*

Befana the Housewife, scrubbing her pane,
Saw three old sages ride down the lane,
Saw three gray travelers pass her door—
Gaspar, Balthazar, Melchior.

"Where journey you, sirs?" she asked of them.
Balthazar answered, "To Bethlehem,

For we have news of a marvelous thing.
Born in a stable is Christ the King."

"Give Him my welcome!"
Then Gaspar smiled,
"Come with us, mistress, to greet the Child."

"Oh, happily, happily would I fare,
Were my dusting through and I'd polished the stair."

Old Melchior leaned on his saddle horn.
"Then send but a gift to the small Newborn."

"Oh, gladly, gladly I'd send Him one,
Were the hearthstone swept and my weaving done.

"As soon as ever I've baked my bread,
I'll fetch Him a pillow for His head,
And a coverlet too," Befana said.

"When the rooms are aired and the linen dry,
I'll look at the Babe."
But the Three rode by.

She worked for a day and a night and a day,
Then, gifts in her hands, took up her way.
But she never could find where the Christ Child lay.

And still she wanders at Christmastide,
Houseless, whose house was all her pride,

Whose heart was tardy, whose gifts were late;
Wanders, and knocks at every gate,
Crying, "Good people, the bells begin!
Put off your toiling and let love in."

Robert Penn Warren

## THE LITTLE WHITE HOUSE

The sun of July beats down on the little white house.
The pasture is brown-bright as brass, and like brass sings,
But I stand there, the hills shudder blue and
withdraw into their dazed distance,
Like paranoia. And the child's cry comes from the house.

Tell me, O where, in what state, did I see the little white house
Which I see—and the wax-wing's gold beak slices
the blue cedar berry,
Which is as blue as distance. The river, far off, shrinks
Among the hot boulders, no glister, looks dead as a discarded
snake-skin scrubbed off on stone. The house

Swims in the dazzle of no-Time. Like joy, the child's cry—
yes, listen—comes from the house.

W. H. Auden

## CHORUS OF ANGELS

Unto you a Child,
A Son is given.
Praising, proclaiming
The ingression of Love,
Earth's darkness invents
The blaze of Heaven,
And frigid silence
Meditates a song;
For great joy has filled
The narrow and the sad,
While the emphasis
Of the rough and big,
The abiding crag
And wandering wave,
Is on forgiveness:
Sing Glory to God
And good-will to men,
All, all, all of them.
Run to Bethlehem.

Paul Engle

## CHRISTMAS

In that dark season when all green things die
Christ gave his first live human cry,
Winter that kills the leaf and piles the snow
Brought the small Son of life to grow.
Recall, in the freezing touch of time, men told
That God became a living Child and shook with cold.
Now through our cities bells in their rocking motion
Call to this day their bronze devotion.
Now look! The air, as if the great sky fell,
Shakes all around us. Like a bell
Hung out in glittering space, the whole live earth
Swings and rings in the stars to praise one little birth.

Winfield Townley Scott

## POEM AT CHRISTMAS

The lilac bushes were small with winter.
Rain-repeated, the abacus of barberries
Ran red, ran red above the smoking snow
And the green chickweed where it winked.
Low to the ground, fog hovered and blew and shifted.
The house we passed was three miles from the last
And, as it turned out, three miles from the next.
A back road between cold-blackened pines
On a cellar of a morning near December's end.
Nobody visible at the house. My question was
Whom were all the Christmas signals for—
The candles in the windows and the doorwreath
Ribboned to render hemlock a gay creation?
At most a stranger or two passed once a day,
Like us, in a moment passing. For us, then?
Yes, if we happened by. But of necessity
First for the mingled joy of decoration
And whoever made it. How else could it be?

Karl Shapiro

## CHRISTMAS TREE

Because the tree is joyous and as a child
Lovely in posture, fresh as wind to smell,
Bearing clear needles like a coat of hair,
    And is well-combed and always mild,
        And stands in time so well,
And strong in the forest or beside a tomb
Looks over time and nature everywhere—
Lift it up lightly, bring it in the room.

And for the adoring man, and long ago
The adoring man who was obscure and clean,
Bring in the tree and stand it on the block.
    He felt that he was free to go;
        He stood beneath the green.
Going was freedom, freedom under the tree,
Freedom before the last crow of the cock,
And life exchanged to keep his freedom free.

Summer is sweet because it brings outside
The warmth of houses and the heated air;
We lie on grass as on a delightful rug.
    Christmas brings winter like a bride
        Indoors with white to wear.
The tree looks normal in the house; it grows
Swiftly into the floor; the children hug
The visitor with his dark and pretty clothes.

Silver and gold and mirror-bright and red,
Now hang the egg-shell baubles on the bough

With tinsel hair as shimmering as a dress,
  And one white star upon his head,
    Proud as a Roman now;
And toys, the miniature instruments of pride,
Lay underneath with packages to bless
The material kingdom of the eternal bride.

Between the acquisiton and the prayer
These stand more human for the common days;
The fir, the family, and the pungent wreath
  And one poinsettia like a crimson flare.
    I think the history of praise
Is central in this present-flowering green
That breathes on little children underneath
And keeps them like the infant Nazarene.

John Frederick Nims

## CHRISTMAS TREE

This seablue fir that rode the mountain storm
Is swaddled here in splints of tin to die.
Sofas around like toads of velvet swarm
And spidery cabinets glitter with flat eye,
For lacquer in the branches runs like rain
And resin of treasure starts from every vein.

Light is a dancer here and cannot rest.
No tanagers or jays are half so bright
As swarms of fire that deep in fragrance nest
In jungles of the gilt exotic night
Where melons hang like moonstone. White above
Rises that perfect star, the sign of love.

On carpets' fairy turf, in rainbow dark,
Here once the enchanted children laid their heads,
Reached for the floating moon above the park,
And all their hopes were simple blues and reds.
Beneath the electric halo, none could see
Swords in the ankle of the victim tree.

Each named a patron star: Arthur said green
For August in the country; and Betty blue
For swinging and the Florida surf; while Jeanne
Decided gold. One horoscope was true:
The star of Donald low and lava-red—
Impetuous Donald, in Australia dead.

Our lives were bound to sorcery and night.
Zodiacs crumble on the boughs of rust
For every child is gone. Some burned too bright
And now lie broken in the bins of dust;
And some, a fortunate few, adventured far
And found assurance in the perfect star.

William Stafford

## DECEMBER TWENTY-FIVE

The date is ashamed. After all these years
to come to this! The bells deny
themselves, in a hurry to have a new trial. Wrong!—
Christmas was one day and not again.
The only thing that lasts is when you die.

Clocks may cross themselves: they are right just once,
no matter how often they assert a return;
and our sky knows this, no matter what bells, what song
Still, the next thing leads toward the last, wherever
that is, and nothing is right so far, we learn

From the bells. Well, any judgment, if it is right,
honors its day; and sight depends on the eye
to bring truth. So go ahead—ring the bells long
all over the world: maybe they will sound, after all,
this time, in the right part of the sky.

Chad Walsh

## LOCK THE DARKNESS IN

God is abroad tonight.
Let all good people stay indoors
While, map in satchel, He explores
The city of His sight.

Pull down the window shade,
For it is best to picture only
The point of light that hovers lonely
In alleys that we laid.

He knocks on door to door
But cannot knock at all there are.
The city reaches very far.
Hold your head firm to the floor.

Sometimes by waiting, win.
Or win at least a night's reprieve.
And with the dawn He'll surely leave.
But lock the darkness in.

Thomas Merton

## CAROL

Flocks feed by darkness with a noise of whispers,
In the dry grass of pastures,
And lull the solemn night with their weak bells.

The little towns upon the rocky hills
Look down as meek as children:
Because they have seen come this holy time.

God's glory, now, is kindled gentler than low candlelight
Under the rafters of a barn:
Eternal Peace is sleeping in the hay,
And Wisdom's born in secret in a straw-roofed stable.

And O! Make holy music in the stars, you happy angels.
You shepherds, gather on the hill.
Look up, you timid flocks, where the three kings
Are coming through the wintry trees;

While we unnumbered children of the wicked centuries
Come after with our penances and prayers,
And lay them down in the sweet-smelling hay
Beside the wise men's golden jars.

Robert Lowell

## CHRISTMAS EVE UNDER HOOKER'S STATUE

Tonight a blackout. Twenty years ago
I hung my stocking on the tree, and hell's
Serpent entwined the apple in the toe
To sting the child with knowledge. Hooker's heels
Kicking at nothing in the shifting snow,
A cannon and a cairn of cannon balls
Rusting before the blackened Statehouse, know
How the long horn of plenty broke like glass
In Hooker's gauntlets. Once I came from Mass;

Now storm-clouds shelter Christmas, once again
Mars meets his fruitless star with open arms,
His heavy saber flashes with the rime,
The war-god's bronzed and empty forehead forms
Anonymous machinery from raw men;
The cannon on the Common cannot stun
The blundering butcher as he rides on Time—
The barrel clinks with holly. I am cold:
I ask for bread, my father gives me mould;

His stocking is full of stones. Santa in red
Is crowned with wizened berries. Man of war,
Where is the summer's garden? In its bed
The ancient speckled serpent will appear,
And black-eyed susan with her frizzled head.
When Chancellorsville mowed down the volunteer,

"All wars are boyish," Herman Melville said;
But we are old, our fields are running wild:
Till Christ again turn wanderer and child.

Gwendolyn Brooks

## CHRISTMAS AT CHURCH

The organ thunders, murmurs, is complete,
  Is hallowed, melts in mysteries.
No more the troubles of the day or dusk
When music is a leaning wall of peace.

We abide in beauty. Beneath high-vaulted glory
The Christmas message is a Medicine.
A healing lotion for offended eyes.
An ointment for the ache that freezes in.

This is our refuge and our Strengthener,
To gird us, spur us back into the flame
And steam. Our forces, faith and confidence.
Our guide, the superstructure of a Name.

Richard Wilbur

## A CHRISTMAS HYMN

A stable-lamp is lighted
Whose glow shall wake the sky;
The stars shall bend their voices,
And every stone shall cry.
And every stone shall cry,
And straw like gold shall shine;
A barn shall harbor heaven,
A stall become a shrine.

This child through David's city
Shall ride in triumph by;
The palm shall strew its branches,
And every stone shall cry.
And every stone shall cry,
Though heavy, dull, and dumb,
And lie within the roadway
To pave his kingdom come.

Yet he shall be forsaken,
And yielded up to die;
The sky shall groan and darken,
And every stone shall cry.
And every stone shall cry
For stony hearts of men:
God's blood upon the spearhead,
God's love refused again.

But now, as at the ending,
The low is lifted high;
The stars shall bend their voices,
And every stone shall cry.
And every stone shall cry
In praises of the child
By whose descent among us
The worlds are reconciled.

Vassar Miller

## CHRISTMAS PEACE

Sleep, my beloved, under the hay,
Under the straw, under the snow,
Under the wings of the dark and the day,
Of the meadowlark and the crow.

Sleep, my beloved, under the straw,
Under the snow, under the hay,
Under the long arms of grace and of law,
With a lullaby and a ballet.

Sleep, my beloved, under the snow,
Under the hay, under the straw,
Under the sky and earth below,
The same light that the shepherds saw.

Philip Booth

## UNCLE CHRISTMAS

Christmas is like a dentist coming for breakfast,
arriving (before the family has brushed) with presents
wrapped by professionals, riddled with family jokes.

The children, who pray release from daily check-ups,
have loved him for lollypop weeks. Braced by tinsel,
they empty their socks to hang for this fat uncle:

he promises pearls, if his nieces, toward this one day,
will grace their meals and promise to fight decay.
You'd think it was his birthday, the way we light

old candles, and set up ritual equipment all night.
Even before the streetlights dim, we wake to welcome
his coming: this gifted doctor descended into The Home

(a human bazaar more bizarre than Persians or Turks).
But this is one day when Dentistry actually works:
we breakfast on prophylaxis, lifted, together,

above the bad breath which corrupts our most loving acts.
The children love him. Only we parents (for Christ's sake)
fear the price of this day he extracts.

Bruce Cutler

## DECEMBER TWENTY-FIFTH ON THE RIO GRANDE

It is what rises, draws together, grows
around an appetite of dust, breaks out
along the pewter facings of the air

what falls through roaring atmospheres of light

what greens mesquite, humps the bunch grass

what drags itself across the face of flint
and sinks in mountain seams of sulphur

what drives itself through iron, through gold, and dow
to tilting marble beds above the dikes
of final lava. and then returns,
takes back each crystal filament, sweats along
the hard saguaro root, wakens the grub,
drums the sleeping prairie dog to deeper dark,

bending, bending, until it springs again
through sand, consuming air, gnawing the light

and it is one, one water, one river
flowing out of the jagged banks of birth
flowing under the arches of our years

as it rises, draws together, grows
around an appetite of dust . . .

## COPYRIGHTS & ACKNOWLEDGMENTS



*Acknowledgments are due*

Doubleday & Company, Inc. for "Gates and Doors" by Joyce Kilmer, copyright 1917 by George H. Doran Company; from the book, *Poems, Essays and Letters* by Joyce Kilmer. Reprinted by permission of Doubleday & Company, Inc.; "The Birth" by Don Marquis, copyright 1915 by Harper & Brothers. From the book, *Dreams and Dust* by Don Marquis. Reprinted by permission of Doubleday & Company, Inc.

Harcourt, Brace & World, Inc. for "Christmas Eve Under Hooker's Statue" from *Lord Weary's Castle*, copyright 1944, 1946, by Robert Lowell. Reprinted by permission of Harcourt, Brace & World, Inc.; "Christmas Tree" by E. E. Cummings. Copyright 1925, by E. E. Cummings. Reprinted from his volume *Poems 1923-1954* by permission of Harcourt, Brace & World, Inc.; "Star Silver" from *The Sandburg Range* c 1957 by Carl Sandburg. Published by Harcourt, Brace & World, Inc.; "Christmas Hymn" from *Advice to a Prophet and Other Poems* c 1961 by Richard Wilbur. Reprinted by permission of Harcourt, Brace & World, Inc.; "Journey of the Magi" from *Collected Poems 1909-1962* by T. S. Eliot, copyright 1936, by Harcourt,

Brace & World, Inc., copyright c 1963, 1964 by T. S. Eliot. Reprinted by permission of the publishers.

Holt, Rinehart & Winston, Inc. for "A Christmas Folk Song" from *The Selected Poems of Lizette Woodworth Reese.* Copyright 1926 by Holt, Rinehart & Winston, Inc. Copyright renewed 1954 by C. Reese Dietrich. Reprinted by permission of Holt, Rinehart and Winston, Inc.; "To a Young Wretch" from *Complete Poems of Robert Frost.* Copyright 1942 by Robert Frost. Reprinted by permission of Holt, Rinehart and Winston, Inc.

Little, Brown and Company for "Christ's Birthday" by Emily Dickinson. Copyright 1935 by Martha Dickinson Bianchi. From *The Complete Poems of Emily Dickinson,* by permission of Little, Brown and Company.

The Macmillan Company for "Christmas Carol" by Sara Teasdale. c 1911, Sara Teasdale. By permission of The Macmillan Company; "Star of My Heart" by Vachel Lindsay. Reprinted with permission of The Macmillan Company from *General William Booth Enters Into Heaven* by Vachel Lindsay. Copyright 1913 by The Macmillan Company.

New Directions for "Carol." From *The Selected Poems of Thomas Merton.* Copyright 1946 by New Directions.Reprinted by permission of New Directions.

Charles Scribner's Sons for "Christmas Eve" from *Poems* by Eugene Field, Charles Scribner's Sons; "Sonnets at Christmas, II" (Copyright 1934 New Republic, Inc.; renewal copyright 1962 Allen Tate) by Allen Tate is reprinted with the permission of Charles Scribner's Sons from *Poems* by Allen Tate.

William Sloane Associates for "Christmas Tree" from *The Iron Pastoral* by John Frederick Nims, copyright 1947 by John Frederick Nims, by permission of William Sloane Associates.

The Viking Press, Inc. for "Christmas Morning" from *Under the Tree* by Elizabeth Madox Roberts. Copyright 1924 by B.W. Huebsch, Inc., 1950 by Ivor S. Roberts. Reprinted by permission of The Viking Press, Inc.

"The Ballad of Befana" by Phyllis McGinley, copyright c 1957 by Phyllis McGinley. "Chorus of Angels" by W. H. Auden, copyright c 1944 by W. H. Auden. "Christmas" by Paul Engle, c Paul Engle. "Christmas Eve" by Conrad Aiken, c 1957, Conrad Aiken. "Christmas Tree" by Karl Shapiro, c 1944 by Karl Shapiro. "Dialogue in December" by Mark Van Doren, copyright 1948, by Mark Van Doren. "The Gift" by William Carlos Williams, c 1957 by William Carlos Williams. "To Jesus on His Birthday" by Edna St. Vincent Millay. Copyright 1928, 1955 by Edna St. Vincent Millay and Norma Millay Ellis. "The Lame Shepherd" by Katharine Lee Bates. Reprinted by permission of Dorothy Burgess. "Only an Hour" by Robinson Jeffers, copyright 1941 by Robinson Jeffers. "Poem at Christmas" by Winfield Townley Scott, c 1959, Winfield Townley Scott. "The Snow Fall" by Archibald MacLeish, copyright 1948 by Archibald MacLeish. "The Song of the Magi" by Edwin Markham. Reprinted by permission of Virgil Markham.